Your Essential Handbook for Airbnb Beginners

Valeria A. Chen

All rights reserved. Copyright © 2023 Valeria A. Chen

Funny helpful tips:

Life's tapestry is woven with threads of joy, sorrow, love, and loss; embrace its intricate design.

Prioritize customer service; satisfied customers often lead to repeat business and referrals.

Your Essential Handbook for Airbnb Beginners : Unlock the Secrets to Success with Expert Tips and Tricks for Mastering the Airbnb Marketplace

Life advices:

Rotate between different literary movements; from Romanticism to Modernism, each offers unique stylistic and thematic concerns.

In the galaxy of relationships, value the stars that shine consistently in your life.

Introduction

This is a comprehensive handbook that walks individuals through the process of becoming successful Airbnb hosts. The guide provides step-by-step instructions, tips, and strategies to help hosts create a compelling listing and deliver an exceptional guest experience.

The guide starts by emphasizing the importance of building a solid foundation for hosting on Airbnb. It includes sections on writing an eye-catching listing title, creating an inspiring listing description, and capturing high-quality listing photos that attract potential guests.

Accuracy is highlighted as a crucial factor, encouraging hosts to provide honest and detailed descriptions of their accommodations and to establish clear house rules for guests.

Maximizing profits is another essential aspect covered in the guide. It includes strategies for pricing, managing availability, and leveraging additional services or amenities to enhance the listing's appeal.

To optimize their listings, hosts are advised to use relevant keywords, create a guest-friendly guidebook, and offer a thoughtful welcome book to help guests navigate their stay smoothly.

Effective communication is emphasized throughout the guide, from engaging with potential guests in conversations to providing helpful information when guests arrive.

The guide also covers the practical aspects of hosting, such as staging the home and preparing for guest check-in. It provides insights into maintaining a clean and inviting space and handling unexpected situations that may arise during a guest's stay.

For hosts who plan to manage multiple listings or want to expand their hosting business, the guide offers advice on scheduling, building a team of reliable assistants, and using the right tools to streamline operations.

Overall, this book equips potential hosts with the knowledge and tools they need to create a successful and enjoyable experience for both themselves and their guests. It serves as a valuable resource for anyone looking to enter the world of short-term rentals and hospitality.

Contents

Action 1: Build Your Foundation 1
    Write A Stellar Listing Title 6
    Write An Inspiring Listing Description 8
    Your Persuasive Listing Photos 14
    Accurate Descriptions 16
    Establish House Rules 18
    Maximize Your Profit 20
    Optimize Your Listing 32

Action 2: Enhance The Guest Experience 38
    Your Neighborhood Guidebook 38
    Your Guest Welcome Book 41
    Your Conversations 45
    When Your Guest Arrives 55
    Staging Your Home & Greeting Your Guest 56
    House Cleaning 60
    Handling The Unexpected 74
    Guest Checkout 78
    Cleaning and Changeover 82

Action 3: Assemble Your Tools 83
    Your Schedule 83
    Your People 88

Action 1: Build Your Foundation

Let The Competition Begin

Did you know there are over 2.3 million properties listed on Airbnb? The popularity of Airbnb has created a lot of competition. When travelers enter a search they can view pages and pages of properties. High quality pictures are - without a doubt - what grabs their attention and showcase your property. You cannot underestimate the importance of professional quality photos. After the photos, it's up to your description to tell and sell. If you don't succeed at getting your property in their mind's eye, they'll move on to the next property. That's why your listing must be organized and well written, so that travelers can easily read the information they're looking for. You want to capture their attention so they don't move on to the next listing. I'm going to show you exactly how to do that here. By the end of this section, you'll have an organized, well written listing description that will compel travelers to want to learn more about it.

Let The Conversation Begin

Once a traveler lands on your listing page, the conversation begins. Think of your listing description as the beginning of a conversation, rather than a transaction. Conversation is the key to building genuine trust and making true connections. Rather than writing to a mass audience, imagine that you're sitting across a table telling a friend about your home. Use a friendly, personal tone that tells a story. You're painting an inviting picture that will show travelers the experience they will have in your home. But remember to keep it real. You don't want it to be misleading in any way. Overselling leads to unhappy guests and negative reviews. Instead, describe some of your favorite parts of your home and why. Talk about what other people have said they enjoyed while staying there.

"Disappointment equals expectation minus reality."

- Chip Conley, Airbnb's Head of Global Hospitality & Strategy

Write An Engaging Personal Profile

Although Airbnb has become more widely accepted, there's always some uncertainty when dealing with people you don't know. A good host profile breaks down barriers and provides a comfort level with both you and the traveler.

Your Profile Photo

Make sure your profile photo is well lit, clearly shows your face and offers a welcoming smile. You want to appear friendly and approachable.

Your Description

This is your first impression to the traveler. What would you say if you were introducing yourself in person? Help travelers get to know a little about you and why you love your neighborhood. Describe some of your interests and why you like to host or travel. Add some fun facts about yourself. It can help guests feel they know you better if they know a bit about your work or where you went to school. What do you like to do in your spare time? What makes you a good host? Where are you from?

Get Verified

Be sure to use the Verified ID feature on Airbnb. Provide as many identity verifications as possible, such as email address, social media, and valid physical identification. This improves your trustworthiness to the online community.

Here are some example profile descriptions:

"I'm a cosmetics industry executive turned full-time rancher. I love animals and love being on my ranch, hosting guests that will enjoy privacy, open space and outdoor fun."

"I'm a life-long Southern Californian and Los Angeles beach lover. I enjoy visits to Venice Beach, going to the local restaurants, and bike riding on the boardwalk. I take pride in my property and always respond to guests needs. I live in the building, so I interact with guests directly – from key exchanges, to cleaning, to questions, and anything in between."

"Native Californian, tech geek, surfer and outdoorsman. I love great food and cocktails. I know where to send people for a real local's experience. I love sharing travel destinations and adventures."

Now It's Your Turn….Write Your Engaging Personal Profile

Worksheet #1

In the following exercise, I've provided cues to help you easily write an impactful personal profile. <u>You'll find an electronic version of this worksheet in the Library of Templates. Click the link to download the files.</u> Answer the questions, and then transfer your final version to your listings.

Perfect Host Process™ - Worksheet #1

Write Your Engaging Personal Profile

Instructions: Complete the 3 steps below to write your own personal profile. Simply answer the questions, and then transfer your final version to your listings.

Step 1: Give yourself a descriptive label:

I'm a….
(Native Texan, Accountant, Surf bum, Wine Enthusiast)

Step 2: What do you like to do in your free time?

who likes to…
(cook, hike, work in my garden)

Step 3: How does this relate to your hosting? Why you like to host?

this makes me a great host because…
(I know the best hiking trails in town; I love sharing what the Seattle area has to offer)

Write A Stellar Listing Title

This is your property's first impression to the world. It has one goal. To make people click on it to learn more about it. What will make your property stand out from all the others? After the awesome photos, it needs to say enough to make them interested. From there, the rest of your listing will do the work.

So when deciding on your listing title, think about what people would especially like about it. It's not enough to say, "2 Bedroom, 2 Bathroom Cottage." You need to be more specific and descriptive. You have 50 characters to make an impact. But keep in mind, they may only see the first 20 characters of your title when browsing the results. Many people make the mistake of wasting valuable space by including the city name. Travelers already know the city they entered in their search - so don't include the name of the city in your title. But, DO use a related location fact that would create appeal. Is it located near any major destinations or landmarks? Are there any special benefits of your location? What do most people want when they travel to your area?

For example:
"Modern + Cozy Suite Near Downtown/Stadiums"
"Stylish One Bedroom, One Block from Space Needle"
"Relaxing Laguna Studio! Ocean Front!"
"Comfortable Loft in the Gaslamp with Parking"
"Family Friendly Avalon Penthouse"
"Sunny Studio Apartment in the Heart of Capitol Hill"
"Swanky Downtown Studio 14th & U"
"Renovated 1917 Craftsman Bungalow, Near Farmer's Market"

Now It's Your Turn….Write Your Stellar Listing Title

Worksheet #2

In the following exercise, I've provided cues to help you easily write an attention getting listing title. Simply answer the questions, and then transfer your final version to your listings.

Perfect Host Process™ - Worksheet #2

Write Your Stellar Listing Title

Instructions: Complete the steps below to write your own listing title. Simply answer the questions, and then transfer your final version to your listings. Note: Make the most of the first 20 characters, as that might be all the guest sees on a search result!!

Step 1: Decide on a one word adjective that describes your home:

(i.e. modern, stylish, family-friendly, sunny)

Step 2: What type of home is it?

(i.e. one bedroom apartment, studio, 3 bedroom house)

Step 3: What is it's special appeal or benefit?

(i.e. near Stadiums, ocean front, view of the pier)

Write An Inspiring Listing Description

Through your description, transport travelers to what their vacation would feel like. Have empathy for travelers and walk in their shoes. Describe the experience they will have at your home, rather than simply listing the features. Organize your description room by room. Take them on an imaginary tour. Use bullet points whenever possible to make it easy for travelers to scan your page and pick out information.

Be very precise when describing the unique appeal of your property. Focus on what makes your place different from others - just as you did when crafting your listing title. Is it convenient to a major destination? What are the unique advantages of staying at your home? For example, do you offer free parking in an area where parking is a challenge? Do you have bikes that your guests can use? Do you have an outdoor hammock in a relaxing spot? Even if your space is simple and modest, you can create a unique one-of-a-kind experience that attracts guests and welcomes them to your neighborhood. You can offer home baked scones and local coffee, or local craft brews representing your town. Some hosts provide soft, spa-like robes for guests to relax in. If you already have some reviews, notice what past guests liked about your home. Use their comments in your description. Be creative to stand out from the crowd!

Take a look at a description below. It gives you the facts, but it's very basic and offers little personality. There is nothing about it that helps you envision what staying there would feel like.

"This is a one bedroom apartment with a view of the city. There is a living room, a fully equipped kitchen with dishwasher, and a dining table that seats 8 people. The master bedroom has a king size bed, and the living room has a full size sofa bed, with a flat screen TV. There is a private patio right outside the entrance. The marble accented bathroom has a bathtub and shower. A large capacity, in unit washer/dryer is also provided for your convenience."

Let's see how this same description can be transformed to be more compelling. Notice how it comes to life by linking the facts to vivid experiences, as if you were physically walking through the home - room by room.

You'll enjoy walking into this private one bedroom garden flat through its own separate entrance. With all its amenities, you'll automatically feel right at home.

Living Room
Walk into the expansive living room with a full window wall that looks out to a landscaped patio and view of San Francisco City Hall. It features:
- A pull out sofa bed with full size mattress
- 52" flat screen TV with Comcast's premium package

Kitchen & Dining
The living room opens up into the gourmet kitchen and dining area, where you can enjoy a quiet dinner cooked at home, or delivered from one of our many neighborhood restaurants. Or join the locals and walk to Falletti's one block away. On Sundays, walk to the local Farmer's Market one block away and pick up your favorite fresh produce. The kitchen and dining area feature:
- Dishwasher
- Dining table with seating for 8 people
- Fully equipped kitchen with everything you need to cook meals at home

Bedroom/Bathroom
After a busy day in the city, soak in the bathtub and fall asleep in the quiet and restful bedroom. It offers the best in luxury:

- Tempur-Pedic king size bed
- 100% Egyptian cotton sheets
- Blackout shades
- Carrera marble bathroom
- Quartz countertop
- Glass shower doors
- Luxurious DXV shower head
- Shower and bathtub

Laundry
- Commercial size Maytag washer and dryer
- Steam refresh cycle to refresh your business or cocktail clothes

Do you see how helpful it is to make you feel like you're there? Notice how you can picture yourself using the amenities. This description helps you imagine exactly how the home's location and special features will make your trip a pleasant experience.

Now It's Your Turn….Write Your Inspiring Listing Description

Worksheet #3
In the following exercise, I've provided cues to help you easily write an engaging listing description. Answer the questions and use the senses to bring your description to life. You'll find an electronic version of this worksheet in the Library of Templates. Click the link to access the files.

Perfect Host Process™ - Worksheet #3

Write Your Inspiring Listing Description

Instructions: To write your own listing description, answer the questions below. Use the senses to bring your description to life. When you're finished, you can transfer your final version into your listings.

Step 1: Write your introductory sentence using your listing title:

From the moment you arrive at this_____(i.e. spacious one bedroom apartment) you'll feel right at home.

Step 2: Give the location highlights:

During your stay, you'll especially love that you can

Ex: walk to Golden Gate Park, see the pier, walk directly to the shuttle service

-
-
-

Step 3: Take travelers on an imaginary tour of your home:

You'll enter this home through the
Ex: courtyard garden, landscaped patio, desert themed walkway,

Living Area:
Enter the main living area and you'll immediately notice:

Features:

-
-
-

Describe the experience when you walk in the room.

Ex: you'll love the view of; take an afternoon nap on the couch, relax in front of the fireplace

Kitchen/Dining Area:

You'll enjoy making meals in the kitchen with its ***(Ex. Cuisinart Food Processor, gourmet cookware, Vitamix blender, Keurig coffee maker, table in front of the fireplace.)***

-
-
-
-

Bedrooms:

Sink into bed after a day_____***(Ex. touring the city, on the beach)***. You'll love :

-
-
-
-

Bathrooms:

You'll feel _____ ***(Ex. relaxed, rejuvenated)*** from the :

-
-
-
-

Laundry:

You'll enjoy the convenience of _____ ***(Ex. private laundry, common area laundry)*** that offers :

-

-
-
-

Outdoor Areas:
Enter the _____ *(private or common area)* _____ *(Ex. patio, backyard, roof deck)*, which is located _____
(right outside your door, across from the property)

Where you'll enjoy: *(Ex. having a family BBQ, reading on the lounge chairs)*
-
-
-
-
-

Neighborhood Highlights:
Take advantage of *(i.e. LA's finest restaurants, the latest concerts, the area's best surfing)*:
-
-
- Browse my Airbnb Neighborhood Guidebook for more local tips!

Potential Problems:
Are there any potential issues you need to tell your guests about?

(Ex. Construction noise, parking limitations, anything that may be out of service)

Your Persuasive Listing Photos

Travelers will look at photos before anything else when searching through listings. They will literally make or break the decision on booking your home. If you have beautiful photos, you will attract more eyes to your page. Don't assume people will read every detail. Quality photos are the best way to highlight what's special about your space and help travelers book confidently. Here are some tips to make sure your photos are top notch:

- If at all possible, have **professional photos** taken. The bookings you will receive will make it well worth the investment. Airbnb offers free professional photography in some areas. If it's offered in your area, it can take over a month to get a photographer, so be sure to take advantage of it right away!

- **The more photos the better!** Travelers will spend more time on your listing if you have a lot of pictures. Show a variety of shots and scenes giving them a complete idea of what your home is really like.

- Write **detailed captions** for each photo.

- Take pictures **during the day**, turn on all the lights and let as much natural lighting in the rooms as possible. The first hour of sunlight and the last hour of sunlight are considered the best time of day to take pictures outside.

- **Remove all clutter.** It will create a more inviting and welcoming impression. Unnecessary clutter is distracting and prevents people from imagining themselves in your home.

- Add some **welcoming touches** - add some flowers and arrange some magazines on a table.

- Your photos should be a **true reflection of your home** at it's best. Make sure the photos will match what the guests see when they walk in the door. You want your space to look inviting, but don't be misleading.

- **Highlight any special features** you discuss in your description. Include a picture of the barbecue you mention. Highlight a plate of home baked scones and a cup of coffee to show that you offer this in the mornings.

- **Include photos of the outside.** This helps keep guests expectations realistic about what your home looks like on the outside.

- **Include pictures of your neighborhood** to get them excited about their destination. If you're within walking distance of a major attraction, include pictures of that destination. Include pictures of nearby restaurants.

Accurate Descriptions

One of the most common complaints travelers have when giving reviews is when listing descriptions are not accurate. That's why it's critical to explain any potential problems you may be aware of. To do this, you want to provide an accurate description. Make sure you describe anything that may negatively impact their stay. Always remember to manage travelers' expectations with the realities of your home. For example:

"A neighboring historic house is under re-construction and access to the garden area is closed off for now. The apartment unit is very quiet with double-paned, insulated windows, and the bedroom is at the center of the house. That said, there could be noise inside the apartment beyond our control during the usual M-F, 8:00 am - 5:00 pm hours. For this reason, we do not recommend staying with children under 5 who take naps or are light sleepers. If you are an early riser and out visiting the city during the day, this is unlikely to be a problem."

This is one of the easiest ways to ensure you have positive reviews. Travelers do not like surprises! You don't want them imagining your house one way and then experiencing something completely different in person. Providing important details in an organized way saves you time and prevents you from having to respond to complaints and problems later.

Get Feedback From Friends

Sometimes you're so familiar with the details of your home that you inadvertently fail to state an important fact. This causes confusion that you may not be aware of until you get a negative review. That's why it helps to have another person read your listing description before you publish it. Send your description to friends who have been to your home and ask them for their feedback. Was there anything left out that you may have overlooked? For example, a guest once told me he thought our roof deck patio was connected to the unit. He was disappointed because that's what he was expecting. It had never occurred to me that guests may have had that impression. I did not say the roof deck was connected to the unit, but I also did not clearly state that it was not. I didn't intentionally mislead him - but that didn't matter - he was disappointed. After receiving that guest feedback, I updated my listing to state "You will access the roof deck through a separate entrance that is not directly attached to the unit at the opposite end of the building."

Establish House Rules

Clearly stated House Rules are an important tool in setting expectations for your guests. Airbnb has a specific area for your House Rules when creating your listing. You wouldn't want guests who are planning a party to book your home, if your home is not suitable for parties. You should also include a copy of your House Rules in your physical Guest Welcome Book. We'll discuss this in more detail in the next section of this workbook.

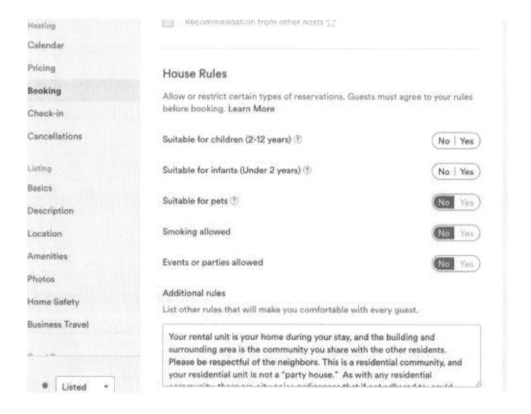

Now It's Your Turn….House Rules Cheat Sheet

Download the House Rules Cheat Sheet in the Library of Templates (click the link to access the files). Customize this form for your own needs. Include this on your Airbnb listing and print the pages to place in your Guest Welcome book. Explain what your guests might need to know ahead of time so that they can make their plans with this in mind. For example, if this is not a party house, if you have age limits for booking, etc.

Maximize Your Profit

As the popularity of Airbnb has increased, more people are jumping on the hosting bandwagon, and this creates more competition. This means your listing must be competitive in every way, including your pricing.

Travel Trends and Pricing

The demand on Airbnb varies by season and tends to correlate with global travel trends. Occasionally, you may notice a drop in the number of bookings and inquiries you receive. When this happens, it pays to do some research. Airbnb hosts in your area may have dropped their prices and are getting all the bookings. Stay informed on the prices of the other listings in your area. Do your own search on Airbnb for similar listings in your area to make sure your prices stay competitive. Here are some other important pricing strategies:

- Airbnb recommends that when you're new to price a little lower until you get some reviews. After you build a few reviews, you can raise your prices in line with your competition.

- Set your rates on a nightly weekly and monthly basis - you may want to provide a discount for longer stays.

- Set Weekend Rates - Demand is higher on the weekends. Compare your rates to your competitors in the area and make sure you are consistent with them.

Create a strategy where you base your pricing on competitive trends, seasons and special events in your area. Some seasonal trends are obvious, such as ski areas in the winter and beach areas in the summer. Other than the seasons, think about what attracts travelers to your area. Is a big game coming to a city near you? Is a major conference coming to your city's convention center? Keep an eye on local event calendars for sporting events, concerts, conferences, etc. If a popular event is coming you may be able to raise your price during those periods. Remember that popular events often book well in advance so it's important to know when they are happening so you can adjust your prices early.

Hotels vs. Airbnb

Be careful when trying to set your rates based on hotel pricing in your area. Airbnb and hotels provide different services. While there will always be a need for the amenities of hotels, the Airbnb experience is different. Travelers may opt for Airbnb over a hotel for usually two reasons: The ability to stay somewhere unique, and the money they can potentially save. If you price yourself like a hotel, you may eliminate as many as half the number of people who may be interested in booking your property.

Is it better to rent your place one third of the time at three times the price, or all the time at one third of the price? The answer is more often at a lower price. People like to save money. So they stay at your reasonably priced Airbnb home, and they leave you a nice review. After a few months, you have a lot of nice reviews. Reviews are what remove the risk of staying at a stranger's house and are the basis to building your Airbnb business.

Be familiar with the hotel rates in your area. This comes in handy when speaking with prospective guests about your pricing. By rationally comparing the value of your home to local hotels, you can highlight the value of your price. For example, a family of four can vacation for a week in a major hotel at $375 per night for 400 square feet with no kitchen. Or they can rent a two bedroom condo with a full kitchen more affordably at $325 a night.

Be careful of leaving your prices too low for too long. If you're finding that you're fully booked for the next 3 months, you might be too low. Keep in mind this rule of thumb:

- At 2-4 weeks out - you should be about 75-90% booked
- At 8-10 weeks out - you should be about 50% booked

You'll notice patterns for your particular area. After several years of hosting, I'm familiar with the pattern for the year. In January and February, I will have fewer inquiries since I'm located in a beach area. My bookings for the winter months are not made as far in advance as they are in the summer months. People visiting my area in winter tend to plan last minute. I know I'll rent during this time, so I set my lower winter rate without any other discounts. As spring approaches, travelers plan their summers. I set my spring rates and summer rates and the summer will become fully booked by the end of May.

Discounts:
In general, only offer discounts if you're uncertain that you'll book the nights. For example, during your off-season it might make sense to offer a special to attract budget conscious travelers. Or, if you have an opening that's only one week away during your peak season, you may fill those nights with lower priced offers at the last minute.

Extra person charges:
How many people does your home sleep comfortably? If you notice guests are often bringing extra people, you may want to charge a fee for each extra person. Make sure you list the maximum occupancy in your rental contract and any extra person charges if they exceed this occupancy.

Finally, don't assume that if you're not getting many bookings that it's because your rates are too high. There maybe other factors involved. Make sure your photos showcase your home and that your listing is well-written and complete. Review your completed Worksheets 1-4 and make sure you followed the steps from the earlier sections of this workbook, and the recommendations from Airbnb.

Avoid confusion between you and your guests. Take advantage of Airbnb's price calculator in your calendar's availability settings allows you to see the price your guests will pay—including taxes, fees, discounts, and more. This helps you understand what travelers actually pay as you establish your prices.

Airbnb Price Tips

It's up to you to determine what you price you want to set for your home. Airbnb aggregates their data based on comparable listings, location and demand and will provide a recommended price. When you set your prices, Airbnb will offer you their price tips directly on your calendar. You my find Airbnb's price tips useful depending on your area. You'll need to decide if it works for you. For example, here are price tips I received from Airbnb for this upcoming Memorial Day weekend.

In this example, the prices Airbnb recommends here are lower than the price I've been getting for the last 3 years on Memorial Day weekend. Perhaps this year will be different due to more competition, so I will consider Airbnb's price tips - but not too far in advance.

Also, if you are a new host, you may want to set your prices lower to make sure you're quickly building your bookings and reviews.

Airbnb Smart Pricing - Lets you set your prices to automatically match demand in your area. You enter your minimum price and maximum price. Airbnb will automatically adjust your price within your parameters based on:
- How many people are searching for listings like yours
- The dates they are searching for
- Whether other listings are getting booked
- Your listing's best qualities

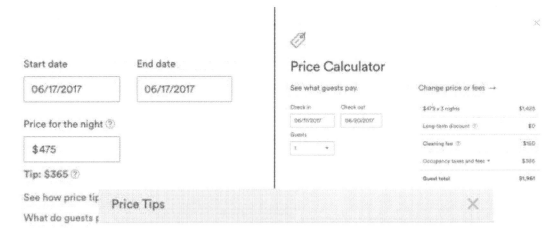

Price Tips

Price tips show you prices that could increase your chances of getting booked.

Top factors affecting this tip:

+$ More than 60 days from today
+$ Day of the week
+$ High demand

Your tips factor in hundreds of attributes that make your listing unique, like travel trends in your area, your location and amenities, past booking history, and the number of people who view your listing page.

Just like traveler demand, price tips can change. Check back often to see if a new tip is available.

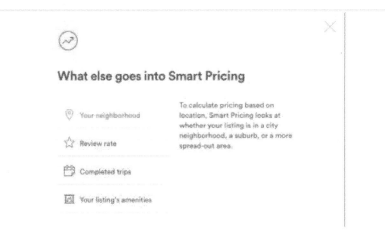

Above are some screenshots of how Airbnb's Smart Pricing works.

The benefit of Smart Pricing is that it automatically adjusts your price for you. I tried Smart Pricing during the winter months, during my slower season, and I found it did not increase my inquiries or bookings. That said, Smart Pricing may be useful for you, and circumstances may be different in your area.

There are also other pricing tools from available from outside vendors to automate your pricing. They search the web for factors that may impact your rental rates to predict demand on a given day, and then generate pricing recommendations specific to your property. Some of the programs sync with Airbnb to automatically update your listing with the latest prices based on demand. Here are some of the more popular automated pricing tools:

- Everbooked
- BeyondPricing
- PriceLabsCo

Airbnb Fees

Host Fees: It's free to set up your listing on Airbnb - you set your price, security deposit and cleaning fee. Guests pay the full reservation fee to Airbnb at the time of booking. Airbnb collects 3% of what you charge guests as a host service fee. Airbnb holds this money and releases it to you by direct deposit 24 hours after the guest checks in, according to the payout preferences you set up in your Account.

Security Deposits: When you set an amount for the security deposit on your listing, the payment details are stored but the guest is not charged for this amount, unless you make a claim. If you notice damage to your property that you believe to be caused by the guest, you must make a claim within 14 days of when the guest checked out, or before a new guest checks in - whichever is earlier. Airbnb will ask you to provide documentation - such as photos of the damage, along with receipts, invoices, written estimates, or links to comparable items that show the actual cash value for repair or replacement. Airbnb will facilitate the communication through the Resolution Center in your Dashboard and collect payment when necessary.

Guest Fees: Airbnb charges guests 6% - 12% on top of the price you charge. The higher the subtotal before taxes and fees, the lower the Airbnb service fee. It helps to know what guests are ultimately paying when setting your prices because it may impact how they perceive the value of your listing price compared to another.

Occupancy tax - In some cities, Airbnb is now collecting occupancy taxes from travelers and remitting them to the appropriate tax authority. Governments differ on the tax rate, how often it's paid and forms required. For more information, visit the website of your city and county and look up "occupancy tax", "hotel tax", or "transient lodging tax."

Calculate Your Potential Profit

Your Airbnb fees are just some of your expenses associated with your business. To determine your profit, you'll need to account for any other costs associated with your business, such as your mortgage or rent payment, property taxes, insurance, housecleaning services, repairs, and any other related expenses.

You'll receive a Form 1099 (U.S. citizens), or a Form 1042 (non U.S. citizens), that will reflect your total Airbnb revenue for the year to be used for income tax purposes. You can also track your earnings at any time by viewing your Transaction History on the Airbnb website. That's why a separate business account is important - you'll be able to keep track of your business income and expenses more efficiently. An accountant can help you determine which expenses are tax deductible. By organizing your expenses and setting a budget, you can accurately determine your financial goals and create a pricing strategy.

Now It's Your Turn....Set Your Budget and Pricing Worksheet #5

Use this worksheet to set your budget and create your pricing strategy. It's important to keep this information updated when you have any changes in costs. You'll find an electronic version of this worksheet in the Library of Templates. Click the link to access the files.

Perfect Host Process™ - Worksheet #5

Pricing for Profit

Use this worksheet to help you plan your pricing strategy. This will help you determine your income needs and set your budget.

Do Some Research:

Visit Airbnb as a Traveler and do a search for properties in your area that are similar to yours - those with the same number of bedrooms and bathrooms. Find ten properties that are the most similar and look at their prices. Then, look at their calendars to see how booked they are in the future. You'll then make your own assessment of pricing vs. market demand

Add up the nightly rental rate of all ten properties, then divide that total by 10. This will give you an average rental rate for properties like yours in your geographic area. You'll need to make adjustments if some properties have a better location, or are more updated, etc.

Income:

Average Nightly Rental Rate for Comparable Homes:

My Expenses:

Mortgage:

Property Taxes:

Other Taxes:

Utilities:

Other Costs:

Your Ideal Price:

Weekend & Seasonal Demand In Your Area:

When is Your High Demand Season?

Are weekends more popular?

When do major events happen in your area?

Note: Open a separate checking account for your vacation rental business. Keep track of your income and expenses using Quickbooks or other business accounting software. You'll be glad you did when tax time rolls around. Airbnb and FlipKey issue Form 1099's for income tax purposes. HomeAway does not issue 1099's. Some local governments require an occupancy tax, hotel tax or lodge tax to be collected. Check on the requirements for your area. Airbnb automatically collects this tax in certain cities, while HomeAway/VRBO does not and leaves this to you.

Optimize Your Listing

There are some general best practices to ensure your Airbnb listing ranks high on searches. Here are some basic tips to keep in mind:

- Determine the **search terms** that would likely be used by your **ideal guests**. Include these search terms in your listing title and description. Also think of appealing keywords **relevant to your area**, such as landmarks, tourist attractions and local events. When you have targeted search terms that match your listing details, your listing will appear higher in the results.

- Make sure you **have high quality photos**. Professional photos are recommended. In fact, the listing websites will let you know if your photos need improvement. Airbnb will sometimes offer free photography session in select cities, so if it is currently offered in your area, definitely take advantage of this free service. Well photographed listings attract more bookings, so it is worth every penny to have professional photos.

- The more **search permutations** your listing satisfies, the more your property will appear in search results. For example, if you set your minimum stay as one night, it increases the flexibility of your listing - which helps it satisfy more searches, leading to more inquiries and bookings.

- Respond quickly to inquiries. The more **active and responsive** you are the websites, the more favorably you are viewed by the algorithms. This means higher ranking when your property meets a traveler's search criteria, more inquiries, and ultimately more bookings.

- **Log-in and update your calendar** regularly. Hosts who update their calendar at least once a month are approximately 70% more likely to get booked than those who allow their calendar to remain out of date for over one month. I update my calendars at least once a week.

- **Keep your listing fresh.** If your calendar is already up to date, just make a few changes to your calendar. Block a few dates, and then free them up again. This action tends to give a nudge to your listing performance. It signals the algorithm to recognize you.

- **Stay competitive** when setting your listing price. We'll discuss pricing in more detail later in this workbook.

- **Turn on Instant Book.** By turning this feature on, your listing will rank higher - but this means that travelers can book your home immediately without any prior review by you. Remember, host cancellations are negatively viewed by Airbnb, and this can hurt your listing performance, so think carefully before turning on Instant Book. Although you set up your parameters with Instant Book, you must be prepared to commit to all bookings in advance. I prefer to communicate with travelers and find out more about who they are and the purpose of their trip before committing to any booking. I'm not interested in unknowingly hosting a frat on spring break. For that reason, I do not use Instant Book.

- Build your list of **reviews**. A history of reviews (especially positive reviews) will increase your listing's performance as time goes on. We'll discuss creating a review strategy later in this workbook.

- **Avoid cancellations.** Always follow through on your agreements with travelers. Airbnb looks unfavorably on host cancellations and may impose penalties on you, such as a blocked calendar. When you cancel bookings it undermines trust, and this will affect your listing performance.

- A **complete profile** with a solid review history shows you take your business seriously and builds your online trustworthiness as a host. Don't leave any areas blank in your profile.

- Create a helpful **Neighborhood Guidebook** within your listing. Host Guidebooks are often used in recommendation lists that are created by Airbnb. If yours is featured, it will increase your visibility on the site. We'll talk more about how to write a neighborhood Guidebook in the next section.

- **Share your listing** and your host profile on **social media.** Search engines place more trust in something that appears more than once. Promote your "host" persona on your social media accounts - make sure to include links to your Airbnb/HomeAway profiles. You can also share your Airbnb wish lists. All of this activity benefits your search ranking across the internet.

- Take advantage of **Airbnb Wish Lists**. When your listing is saved on someone's Wish List, it helps improve your ranking. Encourage people you know who have Airbnb accounts to save your listing on their Airbnb Wish Lists.

Now It's Your Turn....Complete the Airbnb SEO Checklist

Refer back to your Listing Title Worksheet #2.
Refer back to your Listing Description Worksheet #3.

Using the following **Airbnb SEO Checklist**, review your Listing Title and Description. Use the Checklist to make sure you've set your listing up to perform well in possible in searches on Airbnb. You can download this checklist in the Library of Templates. Click the link to access the files.

Airbnb SEO Checklist

1. What search terms would likely be used by your ideal guest? Make sure these terms are included in your description and title.

2. What are appealing keywords relevant to your geographic area? These could be landmarks, tourist attractions and events. Include these terms on your description and title.

3. Is your profile complete? Do you have every section filled in?
_____yes_____no

4. Do you have high quality photos? Do you have enough photos?
_____yes_____no

5. Does your listing match as many search permutations as possible? Based on your hosting preferences, how can you match the most searches as possible. For example, a one night minimum stay would match more searches than a four night minimum. Turning on Instant Book makes your listing very flexible._yes_no

6. Are you able to respond to guest inquiries? Have you downloaded your website's apps so that you can respond on the go?
_____yes_____no

7. How are you updating your calendar? You should update it at least once a week. Block a few dates, and then unblock them. This will nudge the algorithm to recognize you.

8. Are your prices competitive? If you're a new host, set your prices lower to start out.
_____yes_____no

9. Are you making sure you build your trust worthiness by avoiding cancellations?
_____yes_____no

10. Are you sharing your listing on your social media accounts?
_____yes_____no

11. Are you building positive reviews? (We'll cover your review strategy in the next section)
_____yes_____no

Action 2: Enhance The Guest Experience

Consumers today value experiences. Successful companies know this. That's why they focus on creating valuable, customized experiences that consumers cannot get anywhere else. Airbnb knows this too. That's why In addition to offering homes, Airbnb now offers "experience packages" hosted by members of the Airbnb community. Travelers can select experiences from categories such as "Food & Drink", "Art & Design", "Lifestyle", "Sports", "Entertainment", "Nature", "Fashion", "Wellness", "Music" and "History." Understanding your guests and what they want in their getaway helps ensure that they will love staying at your place.

Airbnb has designed the search experience to provide listings that match a traveler's established preferences. So this leads to the question, what will your guest experience be? Travelers on Airbnb have come to expect unique experiences and value, so make sure you are meeting and exceeding their expectations. You can do this through your sense of hospitality, the way you interact with your guests and the value you add to their stay.

Your unique knowledge of your neighborhood is part of what makes you valuable to guests.
Guests appreciate you sharing useful resources in the area such as grocery stores and coffee shops - and tips guests wouldn't expect, like where to find the best pastries or yoga classes.

Your Neighborhood Guidebook

Airbnb provides the option for you to publish a Neighborhood Guidebook with your favorite places to eat and explore in your area. It will appear on your listing page and to your guests. Airbnb also uses your tips along with those of other hosts to create lists of popular places in your geographic area. Your guide could be among those featured in the lists - which could lead to considerable exposure for your listing. Travelers can find everything from coffee shops and parks, to secret spots you recommend. As Airbnb continues to emphasize unique experiences, it will become increasingly common for Airbnb guests to expect this type of hospitality from their hosts. By completing your Guidebook, you are offering your guests a unique perspective that is available only through you.

Now It's Your Turn....Complete Your Neighborhood Guidebook

Go to your Airbnb Host Dashboard - Find the tab for your Guidebook. Add your personal tips there. Think of everything you can that would enhance their visit. The little tips are often the most helpful. Remember, guests are looking for a special getaway that is different from staying in a hotel. As an Airbnb Host, you are creating a unique experience for your guest - one that only you can provide.

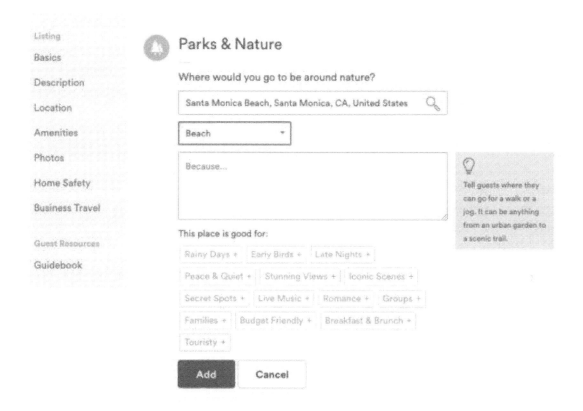

On your Host Dashboard, simply go to your listing page and select "Guidebook" on the left side of your screen. Select the categories you would like to complete. When you type in a place would like to recommend, it will auto fill the location. You can then add your personal experience and why you are recommending it. Once you have completed your Airbnb Guidebook, you can print it. You'll then add these printed pages to your Guest Welcome Book.

Let's now talk about how to create a Guest Welcome Book.

Your Guest Welcome Book

You're familiar with your home, but your guests aren't. Since you know it well, it can help to learn how it feels to be a guest in your own space. If you haven't stayed in your own space already, stay as a guest there yourself so you can have a sense of empathy for your guests. This can help you learn how to make their experience more positive and comfortable. Your Guest Welcome Book can cover everything from how to access the internet, to finding their way around the kitchen, to anything else that will help them settle in and get comfortable right away. In this section, we'll create your Guest Welcome Book. When it's complete, print it and place all pages in a binder with plastic page protectors. Make sure you place the binder in a central location in plain view so that guests see it when they arrive and can refer to it at any time during their stay.

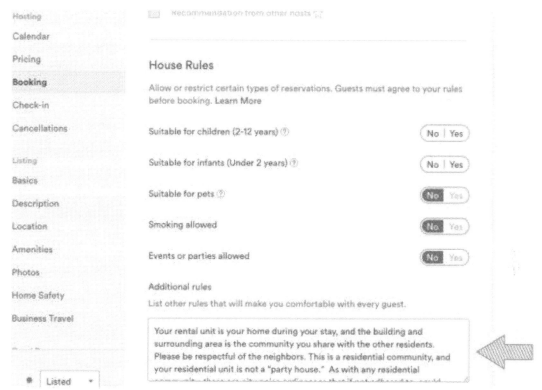

You'll also want to copy and paste your Guest Welcome Book into your listing for guests to have on the go access to this information. On your Host Dashboard, select the Booking tab on the left of your screen.

Scroll down to "House Rules" and look for the "Additional Rules" box. Click inside this box and paste your entire Guest Welcome Book here. Your guests will then have access to your Welcome Book on the go and prior to their arrival.

Now It's Your Turn....Create Your Guest Welcome Book

Access the Library of Templates Bonus Material (click the link to access the files). Download the **Guest Welcome Book Template** and fill in the blanks to customize it for your needs. You can then print these pages to place in your binder to display in your property.

Instructions:
You'll need the following supplies:

- Binder with a clear plastic sleeve on the cover to insert a cover page.
- Plastic page protectors to keep the pages clean.
- Dividers with tabs. Label the tabs with the following titles:

1. Welcome Page
2. Emergency Information
3. House Rules & Guidelines
4. Housekeeping & Supplies
5. Household Equipment
6. Neighborhood Services
7. Groceries
8. Things to Do & Places to Go

- Go to the Guest Welcome Book template in the Library of Templates Bonus Material. Fill in the blanks on each page to customize it using this fillable form.
- Print the completed pages and place them under the appropriate tab in your binder.

- Print the pages from your Airbnb Neighborhood Guidebook that you created on your Airbnb listing. Select the "Print Guidebook" option and place the printed pages in your binder under the tab that is titled "Things to Do & Places to Go."

Your Conversations

By following the Perfect Host Process™ you lay the groundwork for building trust with your guests and a comfortable stay in your home. One of the most important skills of being a successful Airbnb Host is clear communication. From responding to traveler inquiries, answering questions from guests, or corresponding with future guests, you always want to be approachable and welcoming. Understanding their needs helps you make sure that they love staying at your place. Are they looking for peace and quiet? Are they planning a family vacation with kids? Conversations before their stay helps you personalize your hospitality to your guests' needs.

Keep Your Calendar Updated

You may not think of your calendar as a form of communication, but on Airbnb it communicates important information - the dates your home is available for bookings and the dates it is unavailable. More importantly, an updated calendar prevents you from having to cancel any bookings.

To make sure your calendar is current, visit your Host Dashboard and select "Your Listings" then "Calendar." If you list your home on other vacation rental sites, you can choose to synch your calendar with those calendars. To do this, follow the instructions under "Availability Settings." If you know ahead of time that your home will not be available during certain dates, remember to block the dates as "Not Available."

An up-to-date calendar is one of the easiest ways to establish trust with potential guests. You don't want to cancel any reservations or be forced to send an awkward message that your calendar is incorrect. Cancellations are a very bad guest experience. That's why it's important to make sure you do everything possible to prevent cancelling on your guest. For example, Pre-Approve a guest **only** if you are fully prepared to accept the booking. Turn on Instant Book **only** if you are fully prepared to accept all bookings.

Answer Inquiries and Booking Requests Immediately

Your first official conversation happens when you answer an inquiry or booking request from a traveler. Remember to be friendly and approachable in all your conversations, especially this first conversation. **What is an Inquiry?** You receive this message when a traveler is interested in your home and might have some questions. This is your first opportunity to establish rapport. That's why it's important to answer the inquiry immediately. There are several reasons why this is so important. First, it shows warmth and hospitality. Second, the traveler has likely submitted inquiries to more than one host. You don't want to be slow to respond and lose the booking because another host was more responsive. **What is a booking request?** You receive this message when someone has decided to book your home. When you receive a booking request, you can Accept, Decline or send a message if you would like more information.

Set Up Airbnb Notifications

As an Airbnb Host, think of yourself as being "on call." You never know when an inquiry or booking request might come in from across the world. Guests often book with the host that responds first. That's why its important to install the Airbnb app on your phone and set up text and email notifications on your Airbnb account, so that you can respond on the go. You can set this up under "Account Settings" under your profile. Also, make sure the sound is turned up on your phone so that you don't miss a notification. Do whatever it takes to make sure you don't miss notifications on your phone. This is essential to never missing an inquiry or booking. Technically, Airbnb gives you 24 hours to respond to a booking request; however, travelers can change their minds and cancel the request. The slower you are to respond, you increase the chances of losing the booking.

On average, most hosts reply to inquiries within 4 hours and accept bookings within 1 hour.

So why not be better than average? When following the Perfect Host Process ™ you'll want to reply to inquiries immediately and be ready to accept booking requests within an hour. You'll see how easy this is to do through the use of the Library of Templates Bonus Material that you can download by clicking here.

Reviewing the Inquiry or Booking Request

When you receive an inquiry or booking request, double check your calendar to make sure the dates are open. Then read the traveler's message. Most travelers will tell you a little about themselves, who they'll be traveling with and the purpose of the trip. You can usually gain some comfort level through this message. Next, review the traveler's profile. Make sure they have added a photo and notice how the identity was verified. Finally, read through any traveler reviews from other Airbnb hosts. This usually gives me enough information to make a decision. If I still feel like need to learn a little more, I ask for more information. You may need to ask them a few questions to help learn if they would be happy in your space and determine if they are a match. Understanding their travel plans helps you learn what will be important to them.

Accepting or Denying a Booking Request

Once you have made your decision on the booking request, tap the "Accept" or "Decline" button located on the Airbnb Reservation Request message. Should you need to decline the request, you're freeing the traveler to to book another rental. That's why responding within one hour is good customer service.

Choose If You Want To Turn on Instant Book

Instant Book lets you automatically accept reservation requests that fit your pre-set requirements, meaning that you don't need to approve guests before they book - this gives you an excellent response rate in the eyes of Airbnb. But make sure you are prepared to commit to all dates - you don't want to have any cancellations.

Note: Respond to all inquiries and requests! If you let four consecutive reservation requests or booking inquiries expire without responding, Airbnb may temporarily deactivate your listing. They may also deactivate your listing if your response rate is less than 50% across ten bookings.

Keep in mind, if you will be unavailable to host for a certain period of time, you can temporarily pause your listing.

Saving Your Message Templates

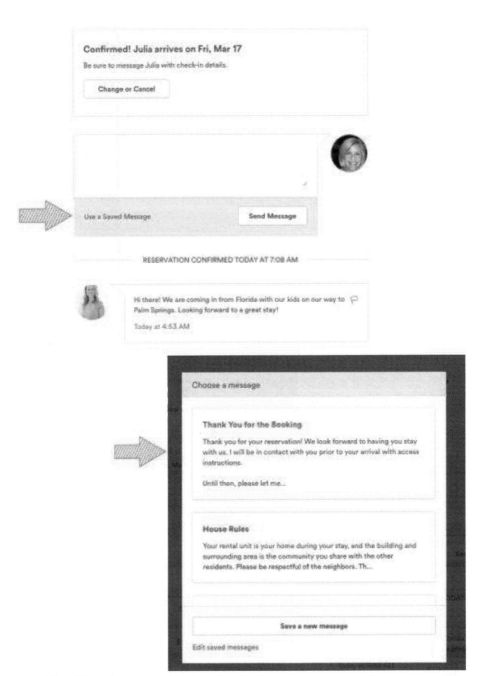

You'll also want to include a personal message with your response. You can create Saved Messages for specific purposes to use every time. For example, save a "Thank You for the Reservation"

message to send to guests immediately after you accept a reservation. For pre-written messages you can copy and paste into your saved messages, refer to the Library of Templates Bonus Material (click the link to access the files).

Using saved messages, you can draft and save the answers to your guests' most common questions. For example, you can type directions to your home once, click save, and it will be ready to send to the next guest.

Preparing For Your Guests' Arrival:

It's important to set up a basic arrival routine for each guest:
- Choose a check-in procedure that works for you
- Decide how guests will access your home, whether you'll be there or not
- Create guidelines for key exchange or pick up and drop off

When you provide clear pre-arrival communication and check-in processes, it will help ensure that your guests will have a stress-free arrival.

Here are some important steps to follow before their arrival day:

- Ask for your guests' travel plans so that you can plan convenient check-in times.
- Send them CLEAR instructions on directions to your home and finding the exact location of the property.
- Send them detailed, precise check-in instructions, so they are not left to guess anything. This includes accessing the keys or entry codes.
- Make sure they know how to contact you on arrival day.
- Use email, messaging and texting to be in contact whenever needed.

In the next section we'll discuss the **Perfect Host Process™ Conversation Sequence.** It will provide you step-by-step messaging that will lead to happy guests and a growing collection of Five Star reviews.

Perfect Host Process™ - Conversation Sequence

Message #1 - Thank You Message/Email Upon Booking

Message #2 - Pre-Arrival Instructions Before Check-In (2 weeks before)

Message #3 - After Check-In Welcome

Message #4 - How is Everything Going? (Halfway Through Their Stay)

Message#5 - Pre-Check-Out Reminder

Message #6 - Thank You & Review Request (Immediately After Check-Out)

Download the Library of Templates Bonus Material (click the link to access the files).

There you'll find templates for each of these messages. Copy and paste these messages into your "Saved Messages"in your Airbnb Host Dashboard.

When Your Guest Arrives

When guests arrive, they are usually tired and preoccupied, so you want to make it easy for them to arrive and immediately feel at home. Create a memorable first impression so when they walk in the door they smile and say, "Wow!" The way you welcome guests can set the tone for their entire stay.

Remember, they've planned on a relaxing and fun getaway. They want it to be special, and you don't want to disappoint! What would make you feel at home right away? Empathize with your guests. In fact, if you haven't stayed in your rental home yourself, you need to do this. Look for anything that needs improvement and change anything that would make it more comfortable and functional.

When to Reach Out To Your Guests:

Guests have different preferences for how they interact. Some will contact you often and others will have very little contact unless they need something. Whether you're there or not, they like to know how they can reach you if they have a question or need any help. It's important for you to stay in touch with your guests throughout their stay. That's why Message #3 and Message #4 are so important. Send Message #3 right after they arrive to find out how everything is going and let them know you're available. If they're staying for five days or more, send Message #4 halfway through their stay to check in on them. Just before it's time for them to check out, send Message #5 and ask them if they have any questions. The Perfect Host™ Conversation Sequence is especially helpful with guests who don't say much. They may be unhappy about something and never say a word to you about it. By having a consistent routine you won't have guests feeling like you aren't available or falling through the cracks if they're more quiet.

Next we'll discuss cleaning and staging your home for your guest's arrival day, as well as welcoming your guest.

Staging Your Home & Greeting Your Guest

Even if you're not there to meet them, you should establish your own greeting routine for your guests. Make sure you're available to answer any questions, especially if you're not there in person. I always plan on responding to messages when I know guests will be arriving. I've learned that following consistent steps for staging my home and greeting every guest the same way every time, ensures things run smoothly. That's why guests are happy when they arrive. This sets the tone for their stay and gets their trip off to a good start. In fact, here are a few screenshots of the types of messages I often receive right after guests arrive.

Oh good! I'm so glad you're happy with it! Enjoy!!!

Feb 7, 2017 via Airbnb SMS

 Thanks for making this feel like home

Feb 7, 2017 via Airbnb SMS

 Been traveling for work for a month and I'm grateful

Feb 7, 2017 via Airbnb SMS

 Ha

Feb 7, 2017 via Airbnb SMS

 My heart burst you have the best laundry set up thanks

Feb 7, 2017 via Airbnb SMS

Making It Extra Special: Ideas That Go Above and Beyond

A thoughtful gesture goes a long way to make them feel welcome. Here are some ideas if you'd like to add a little extra welcome and personality to your home:

Kitchen
- Welcome note
- Coffee with coffee creamers and sweetener
- Fruit bowl

- fresh flowers
- Cookies/candy/chocolate on a plate
- Sweets from a special place in your town
- bottle of wine & 2 glasses
- recipe book & stand
- bottled water in refrigerator
- useful range of small kitchen appliances such as blender, coffee maker

Living/Dining Areas
- Bowls with decorative items
- Set dining table with plates, glasses, etc.

Bedroom
- Items that suggest relaxation and comfort
- Picture above bed
- Fresh flowers
- Throw cushions

Bathroom
- Basket of toiletries
- Spa basket

Laundry
- Basket of special laundry essentials
- Fabric softener
- Laundry soap

House Cleaning

A clean space is a must - clean spaces make guests feel comfortable from the moment they arrive and can show your commitment to making them feel welcome. After a guest's stay, they can specifically rate the cleanliness of your listing and let future guests know what their experience was like. Cleanliness is the most basic requirement. You don't want negative reviews for cleanliness! Cleaning for guests is different than cleaning for yourself. Guests are expecting to find your place looking like the photos on your listing. Every room should be clean, especially the bathroom and kitchen.

Guest Amenities
Most Airbnb guests expect the following basic amenities:

- High Speed Wireless Internet
- Hairdryer
- Shampoo
- Iron/Ironing Board
- Linens and towels
- Soap
- Toilet Paper

Make sure that each of these items are replenished between each guest, so that they are fresh for the next guest. The **Supplies Checklist** that follows will help you keep track of supplies you have on hand and those you need to purchase. If your hire a cleaning service provide this checklist to them so that they can inform you when you need to purchase additional supplies. You can also download this checklist in the Library of Templates (click the link to access the files). You'll also find a **Home Staging Checklist** and a **Six Point Cleaning Checklist** to help you prepare for arriving guests.

Proper cleaning takes time and effort. I recommend charging a cleaning fee and paying a housekeeper or service to clean according to these standards. These tasks should be completed for every new guest. The checklists are useful to make sure that everything is done the same way every time - ensuring the best experience for your guests.

Perfect Host Process™ - Supplies Checklist

Household

- Lockable storage shed or cabinets for any personal items you don't want used (clearly marked Owner's Cabinet)
- Fans/Ceiling fans
- Cleaning supplies for guest use
- windex
- comet
- laundry detergent
- Iron/Ironing board
- Paper towels
- Toilet paper
- Light bulbs

Kitchen

- Kitchen supplies for fully functioning kitchen (use the kitchen yourself to make sure)
- Sufficient plates, cutlery and glassware for the maximum people you accommodate
- Sufficient plastic plates, cutlery and glassware for outdoor use
- Wide range of small appliances such as a blender, food processor, waffle maker, slow cooker
- Cooking pans and cooking utensils (in good condition)
- Large pot for boiling corn or cooking pasta.
- Coffee maker

Living/Dining

- Comfortable seating in living area
- Enough seats for the amount of people who stay there

Entertainment/Recreation

- Board games, decks of cards, toys, books clean and in good condition.
- Check all board games and packs of cards to ensure they are complete.
- Cooler
- Beach chairs, beach umbrella

Perfect Host Process™ - Supplies Checklist, cont.

Bedrooms

- Mattress covers - replace if needed
- Pillows - replace if stained
- Extra linens, pillows and blankets for each bedroom
- Full length mirror

Bathrooms

- Hair dryer
- Bath Soap
- Hand Soap

Safety/Emergency Supplies

- First Aid Kit
- Functioning smoke alarm
- Functioning carbon monoxide detector
- Functioning fire extinguisher

Posted Emergency Sign*

- Clearly marked fire escape route and map
- Local emergency numbers and the nearest hospital
- Emergency contact number for you and a backup person

*Customize and print the Emergency Sign Template located in the <u>Library of Templates</u>.

Supply Closet

- Restock paper products (toilet paper, paper towels, coffee filters, etc.).

- Restock cleaning supplies that you leave for your guests including: all purpose leaner/disinfectant, dishwasher detergent, window-cleaner, furniture polish, floor cleaner, and spot remover for carpets.
- Restock trash bags.
- Replace vacuum cleaner bags and provide back-ups.
- Check brooms and mops to see if they need replacing.
- Be sure you have ample supply of back-up supplies that must be replaced more often, such as extra coffee carafe, back-up TV remote controls, extra pillowcases, extra glassware, etc.

Perfect Host Process™ - Home Staging Checklist

- Curtains open
- A lamp or overhead light on a dimmer
- Ceiling fans on (warm weather)
- No magnets on refrigerator
- Switch on under counter lighting
- Notes placed in strategic places. (i.e., recycling bins labeled, how to use the thermostat, how to operate ceiling fans.)
- WiFi code clearly displayed on a note or in a frame
- Guest Welcome Book placed in a prominent location.
- Local brochures of nearby things to do
- Printed neighborhood map
- Designated key area (i.e., on a hook, or basket on kitchen counter)
- Keys should be labeled as to what they are used for
- Clean and fresh smelling - no overpowering odors that might be unpleasant to some people, or affect allergies
- Fresh towels hanging in the bathroom
- Fresh sheets on the beds
- Folded, nicely presented linens (with no stains or tears)
- Fresh soap in bathrooms and in tubs/showers (Refill liquid soap bottles so they are full; replace used bar soap with a new bar of soap.)
- Laundry soap in laundry area
- No clutter.
- No dust.
- All dishes are clean and neatly put away. (No dishes in the dishwasher.)
- Clear and clean all countertops
- Small kitchen appliances put in cabinets

- Dish towels clean and folded in drawers; don't leave out
- Cleaning supplies available for guest use
- Closet and/or dresser for guest belongings
- Consider a rack for luggage to create space in the bedrooms
- If you use a lockbox, check to make sure keys are there
- Smoke and carbon monoxide detectors are working; replace batteries if necessary
- Declutter dressers, side tables and coffee tables

Perfect Host Process™ - Home Staging Checklist, cont.

- Switch on bedside lamps and side table lamps
- Beds should have attractive, matching linens with plenty of pillows, include extra linens in closets
- Tidy cables in TV areas
- How does the lighting affect the ambience? After dark, does the space feel welcoming and cozy, or dark and unwelcoming? Is there sufficient lighting in living rooms and bedrooms for reading?
- Carpet and rugs free of stains and wear
- Remember to replace anything that looks old or unclean
- Put away personal photos in frames
- Minimal knick knacks

Exterior:

- Curb appeal
- Entryway and walk-up clear of debris, leaves or fallen branches
- plants, hanging baskets, planted pots
- clear of debris
- do screens need cleaning?
- does exterior siding need to be power washed?
- neat and tidy
- tables/chairs arranged nicely
- items to be stored are put away neatly
- clean windows and window sills
- patio furniture and umbrella - no broken or mildewed pieces
- BBQ with cleaning brush - in working order
- Power wash and paint if needed
- Remove stored materials that could be safety risks for children - fertilizer, rodent poison, flammable liquids

Perfect Host Process™ - Six Point Cleaning Checklist

1. Bathrooms:

- Clean, scrub and sanitize showers, bathtubs, vanity, sinks, and backsplashes.
- Clean mirrors.
- Clean and sanitize toilets.
- Polish chrome.
- Wash floors and tile walls.
- Empty wastebasket.
- Replenish liquid hand soap.
- Clean linens: 2 hand towels, 4 washcloths, 2 bath towels per guest and 1 shower mat.

2. Bedrooms:

- change sheets/pillowcases (no stains or tears)
- mattress clean and free of mildew and damp smells
- check for evidence of bed bug activity
- mattress cover in good condition - replace stained or worn ones
- clear area to create space for unpacking
- dust furniture and clean mirrors.
- vacuum floor and under beds
- Check for personal belongings left in drawers and closets.
- Check windows for fingerprints.
- Make sure light bulbs are not burned out.
- Check for wear and tear/stains on pillows, sheets and blankets.
- Wash blankets and comforters after every 10 rentals.

3. Kitchen

- Clean refrigerator inside & out: remove old food

- Clean appliances, counters, cabinets, table, and chairs.
- Clean, scrub, and sanitize sinks, countertops, and backsplashes.
- Clean range top and wipe out inside of oven.
- Clean appliance exteriors, including the inside of toaster and coffee maker.
- Clean inside and outside of refrigerator and microwave oven.
- Wash/mop floor.
- Empty dishwasher, and quickly organize cupboards.
- Restock auto dish detergent, liquid dish soap, coffee filters, and trash bags.
- Put out 2 clean dish towels, and a new sponge.

Perfect Host Process™ - Six Point Cleaning Checklist

4. Living Room Clean, dust, and vacuum.

- Dust window sills and ledges.
- Dust furniture, blinds, picture frames, knickknacks, ceiling fans, and lamps.
- Vacuum carpets or wash floor.
- Vacuum furniture, including under seat cushions.
- Check sofa bed for dirty linens.
- Wash windows on sliding glass doors.
- Empty and clean wastebaskets.
- Be sure to leave clean linens for the sofa bed.

5. Other areas

- Be sure washer and dryer are empty; clean out lint trap.
- Check light bulbs, change if necessary.
- Once per month, change furnace filter.
- Wipe off patio set, clean barbeque grill.
- Notify owner immediately if you notice any damages, missing items, or if the home was left excessively dirty.

6. Monthly Tasks:
Date Last Performed_____

- Spot clean walls, doorknobs, light switches
- Extra dusting of wall art, mirror frames, ceiling fans, etc.
- Clean baseboards
- Steam clean carpets
- Check for signs of bugs or pests
- Replace batteries in smoke detectors and carbon monoxide detectors
- Check pressure gauge on fire extinguisher

- Replace furnace and air filters
- Vacuum vents and behind large furniture
- Vacuum lint trap on the dryer and wash inside of washing machine
- Clean windows
- Wash curtains or clean window blinds
- Guest Welcome Book should be clean and free of stains, creased or torn pages, etc. - replace with fresh pages or a new binder if necessary

Perfect Host Process™ - Six Point Cleaning Checklist

List of any missing/damaged items from this changeover

Date _____

Include details of damaged or missing items.

Other Notes:

Handling The Unexpected

If you've hosted on Airbnb long enough, chances are at one time or another the unexpected will happen. Whether it's a plumbing problem, a lost garage door opener, or disruptive noise from construction, the question is not *if* things will go wrong, it's **when** they will go wrong. The most important part of handling a problem is to be responsive. Always make sure you can be reached. Be available to communicate as needs come up. If you're not there or cannot be available, make sure to provide an alternate contact person in case something comes up.

Apologize Quickly... Among hundreds of guests, things are bound to go wrong at times. I once had a guest who was disturbed by noise from upstairs that was beyond my control. I received this message early one morning:

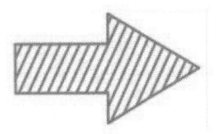

renter. It's after 2 am and the people upstairs have been loud for hours. I suffer from insomnia and can't get any rest on a much needed vacation! Elizabeth

Thu, Feb 2, 6:27 AM

I am so sorry. I just read your message. I have contacted the person upstairs and told him that he is too loud and to stop whatever he has been doing. I would like to make this up to you in some way. I will be in touch later this morning.

Thu, Feb 2, 7:43 AM

I responded as soon as I received the message, so that she knew I cared.

…Then Go the Extra Mile

> Thank you!
>
> Thu, Feb 2, 11:22 AM
>
> I would like to treat you $50 to happy hour. Let me know when/ where you're going and I will call ahead. I recommend the rooftop bar at Hotel Erwin http://mobile.highvenice.com/ They are popular so I would recommend making a reservation. Let me know!
>
> Thu, Feb 2, 1:35 PM
>
> Thank you so much! We have a 6:30 reservation at the bar at the Hotel Erwin.

I then invited them to visit a local popular rooftop lounge for Happy Hour on me. What could have become a terrible review, became a 5 Star Review that has lead to many more bookings.

Ideas for Going the Extra Mile:
- Happy Hour drinks at a favorite local restaurant
- Amazon gift card
- Airbnb credit

Always Follow Up - Check back in with your guests after you have worked to resolve the problem and ask them if the situation has improved. This lets guests know that you sincerely care about their experience.

Guest Checkout

Pre-Checkout Reminder

Just as with welcoming your guest, setting up a consistent routine when your guest leaves makes things run smoothly. Leave a printed **Guest Checkout Checklist** next to your Guest Welcome Book, so they have an easy way to refer to the check-out steps.

The day before they check-out, send your guests a pre-checkout reminder message. This gives you a chance to remind them of your check-out procedures and ask them to tell you about any areas of improvement they noticed. They can either write their feedback on the **Guest Checkout Checklist**, or reply directly to your message. This lets them know that you genuinely want their feedback. If they have any concerns or negative feelings, it gives them a chance to let you know privately - before posting anything on a public review. It gives you a chance to address those concerns, making it more likely that they will then leave you a positive review.

Now It's Your Turn….Send Message #5 Pre-Checkout Reminder
(1 day before checkout)
& Create Your Guest Checkout Checklist

In the Library of Templates Bonus Material, you'll find a fillable form you can customize to create your Guest Checkout Checklist. Print a copy and leave it next to your Guest Welcome Book, so that guests can locate it easily. Even though you may have this listed in other places, many guests will still ask what your checkout procedures are. Having a printed copy for them saves them the effort of asking you what they should do before they leave.

To send your Pre-checkout Reminder use the template for **Message #5**, located in the Library of Templates Bonus Material (click the link to download). You should have also saved this message to your Airbnb saved messages.

Predictable Positive Reviews

One of the essential elements of the Perfect Host Process™ is that you're initiating the conversation, not responding. You're a proactive host, not a reactive host. The grand finale of this process is the Guest Review - it's a key part of building a successful Airbnb business. Your business and the Airbnb community rely on these reviews, and guests rely on reviews when they decide where to book. If you've followed **Perfect Host Process™ Conversation Sequence** we discussed in the previous section, positive reviews will become a predictable result, every time!

When I first started hosting, there would be times when something had gone wrong for a guest, and I was not aware of it. Because they never mentioned it to me, I assumed everything was fine. Then I was blindsided by a negative review. This happened to me more than once, and it's why I created the **Perfect Host™ Conversation Sequence** we've been discussing. By following this formula, you will have very few surprises, if any. Without this level of ongoing communication, you won't always know if guests were unhappy - until they leave you a negative review. You can't rely solely on Airbnb's automated messaging to do this for you.

Immediately after they check-out, thank guests for staying with you and ask them to tell you about any areas of improvement they noticed. This lets them know that you genuinely want their feedback. If they have any concerns or negative feelings, it gives them a chance to let you know privately - before posting anything on a public review. It gives you a chance to address those concerns, making it more likely that they will then leave you a positive review. This final step in the Conversation Sequence will help you build a consistent stream of Five Star Reviews every time:

Now It's Your Turn…. Send Message #6
Thank You & Review Request (Immediately After Check-Out)

Download the template for Message #6, located in the [Library of Templates Bonus Material](click the link to download). Remember to also keep this in your Airbnb saved messages.

It's a simple message that must be sent immediately after check-out:

"Thank you for staying with me. I hope you enjoyed your time in Los Angeles. I work very hard to make sure all of my guests have a wonderful stay. This property is my small family business, and a 5-Star Review goes a long way for us! If you enjoyed your stay and wouldn't mind, could you please write a review about your favorite parts of our home? I would really appreciate it!"

Then, pay close attention the feedback you receive from these messages and from your reviews. It's valuable information you can use it to improve and update your listing. You might find out you need to upgrade your amenities, or update your listing to be more accurate.

Leaving Your Guest a Review

At the same time you send the Thank You message, leave your guests a review. This is another chance to thank them and provide helpful feedback. When you are the first to leave a review, it encourages guests to leave a review for you.

Cleaning and Changeover

Once they have left, use the **Six Point Cleaning Checklist** and **Supplies Checklist** to make sure everything is in order. Make sure to give a copy to your house cleaning service or any other people who help you with guest changeovers.

During the changeover, anything missing or damaged should be documented by you, your house cleaner, or another person you designate. On the last page of the Six Point Cleaning Checklist, you'll find an area to document this information. Keep in mind that Airbnb requires proof of value when making a claim - which would include photos and/or video along with receipts, invoices, written estimates, or links to comparable items denoting actual cash value for repair or replacement.

If you often have back-to-back guests leaving and arriving on the same day, you will need to be strict with your check-in and check-out times. You will avoid a lot of problems if you clearly state your policy in your check-in and check-out instructions. Make sure you allow plenty of time to clean the property and change the laundry. You also need to allow time to deal with any issues that might be discovered during the changeover.

While guests appreciate flexibility in arrival and departure times, you must specify that they ask ahead of time for any changes to the schedule. If I have a day or more free between bookings, and a guest has a later flight or arrives early, I'm more than happy to accommodate late departures and early arrivals at no additional cost. Guests have told me they really appreciate this flexibility which has led to very positive reviews.

Action 3: Assemble Your Tools

Your Schedule

If you have multiple properties, or are managing remotely, it's difficult to be in multiple places at once. That's when automation tools make the difference.

Self Check-In Tools
Airbnb has an option where you can choose "Self Check-In" on your listing - this is highlighted on your listing, which some travelers like. There are a few options available for automating check-in:

1. Electronic Locks
Electronic code locks replace your deadbolt and allow entry via a punch-in code. It also allows you to generate a new code for each guest.

2. Lockbox with Key
This choice is somewhat less secure since you cannot change keys after every guest. Simple combination key boxes are an inexpensive option for ensuring your guests get their keys no matter what time of day they arrive.

3. Smart Locks
These devices use an electronic system which allow property access when it receives a wireless signal (often via Bluetooth) from a verified smartphone. That means you can remotely grant access to a guest a few hours before check-in to keep things really simple.

4. Co-Manager, or Concierge Service
If you prefer to keep the personal touch of greeting upon arrival, you can hire someone else take care of it for you. Vacation rental

concierge companies can also provide welcome tours of your home, carry out security checks and even attend to laundry and housekeeping between guests. Airbnb has the option for you to designate a Co-Host - who would have access to your Airbnb Host Dashboard and messaging.

Airbnb Calendar Settings

Your Airbnb calendar settings have some options that can help you manage your bookings efficiently. For example, some hosts prefer to block time between bookings to prepare for their next guests or manage time for cleaning. To do this you can automatically block a day or two between bookings.

You can also avoid same-day or next-day requests by selecting the appropriate option on your calendar settings.

You can control how far in advance you want to schedule bookings. For example, you can prevent reservation requests that are more than three months in the future, or allow bookings more than a year in advance.

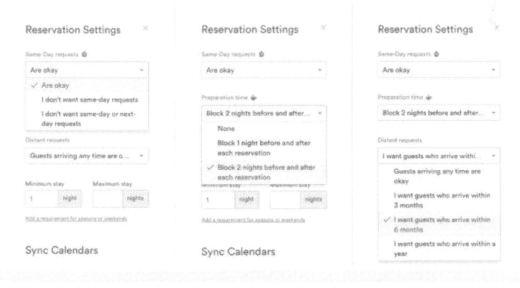

You can use the calendar's "preparation time" feature to automatically reserve up to two days between bookings. You can also adjust check-in and check-out times to leave yourself more time, as well as think ahead and block longer periods of time when you need a break from hosting.

Email Management:
When you receive a message, text or email, it's helpful to ask yourself these questions:

1. Is this from a current guest? If so, it needs to be answered immediately. For all other messages…

2. Can this request be done in two minutes or less?
If the answer is yes, do it immediately.

3. Can it be handled by someone else? If the answer is yes, forward the request to that person.

4. Can this wait? Maybe it is a request that will take longer than 2 minutes, and you can't delegate it to someone else. So you consciously decide to defer it. Add it to your To-Do List and schedule time on your calendar to complete it.

What if the message is not asking you to do anything? Maybe someone is just providing you information. In that case, you need to decide if it's information you might need later. If so, then file it. When in doubt, file it. You can always delete it later. Keep your files simple. I prefer to use one folder labeled "archived". Too many folders gets complicated. Before you know it, you've forgotten where or why you filed it in a certain folder. This leads to procrastination.

Email Management Tools:
Take advantage of the filter rules available to you in your email program. You can create your own rules such as emails from certain

senders, or certain types of emails can be automatically sent to their own folder. For example, once a month, your homeowners association sends you the minutes from the last board meeting. You can set up these emails to automatically go into a "Homeowner's Association" folder. They can stayed queued for you there, still unread. This allows you to prioritize your emails.

There are some email management tools available that are easier to use than email filters. Here are a few:
- **SaneBox** will sort your inbox for you before you even look at it. It can move all the emails you subscribe to, such as newsletters to a special folder you designate. That means the only things you see in your inbox are the important emails that you want, such as personal or professional messages from real people. All the promotions, newsletters, receipts can be sorted for you before you even check your email.
- **UnrollMe** consolidates unsubscribing for you. It segregates out every email that has an "Unsubscribe" link and provides you a list in one email where you can decide whether or not to unsubscribe to each one individually, or just unsubscribe to the entire list. You can elect how often UnrollMe sends you this list.

Identify common requests and create templates for the answers.

You'll notice a pattern in questions that guests will often ask you. When you notice these common questions make sure the information is clearly written in your Guest House Manual or Welcome Book - if you're getting repeated questions on something there is a good chance you have not provided clear instructions, or the information is hard to find. To save time, let pre-written responses answer the questions for you. So when you get one of these common questions or requests, pull up the template, such as "Bike Lock Combinations" You can modify the language to personalize it, and hit send. If I'm responding by email, I have my common responses saved as different email signatures.

If I'm text messaging, I create pre-written text messages and save them in my "Notes" app, and then copy and paste the message I need in the new text.

Your People

Assemble Your Local Team
- Handyman, housekeeper, plumber
- Internet Provider phone number, account number
- TV Cable company phone number, account number
- Local point of contact for guests if you're not close by - friend, neighbor, Airbnb co-host, professional concierge service

Now It's Your Turn…. Your Local Team List Cheat Sheet

_____ _____

Printed in Great Britain
by Amazon